Hidden Purpose

Breeawna Hayes

Dedication

I want to dedicate this book to the Lord. You are worthy.

I want to thank my friend Elizabeth Bennet for always recognizing the potential within me, because of your faithful encouragement this book has come to pass.

I also want to thank my Pastors, Jeff and Summer Hughes and Allen and Kristin Hawes, for their continuous love, wisdom, and leadership.

Thank you to my best friend, Hailée Febres for continually praying for my heart.

I want to recognize my wonderful mother, Shawn Owens–Hayes, for always supporting me in my journey with the Lord. Momma, I love you!

Introduction

YELLOW. In case you were wondering, that's how I say hello. Before you read much more, Yellow! My name is Breeawna Hayes. One morning, during the plandemic, my friend Libby said, "You'll write a book one day." I thought to myself, yeah right! Well, she was right. Here we are friends! Here's just a taste of what it looks like to go to the garden. Let's take the Father's hand and go on a journey. A few things I want you to keep in mind, don't be religious, get out of your head, and ask the Holy Spirit to give you revelation. You are a seed, the Word is a seed, and Jesus himself is the seed. Be willing, and obedient, your purpose is hidden in your submission to His process. Before we were called to anything else, we were called to Jesus Himself. I pray you open up your heart and invite The Father in, cultivating an unbreakable connection. May you be found in Him and remain connected to Him.

Webster's defines the word "process" as: a series of actions or steps taken to achieve a particular end. As believers, the process, or series of actions that we go through is continual. The Bible instructs us to die to ourselves and our natural way of thinking in order to grow and bear fruit. Every believer has the potential to grow. It's what you do with your potential that counts. You'll remain with only potential unless you apply the Word. Potential is the sum of everything we are, which has yet to be revealed or manifest. The potential of a harvest is wrapped in a seed, we must be willing to die. *"Now the parable is this: The seed is the Word of God." - Luke 8:11 KJV.* What happens when you plant a seed into the ground and properly care for it? The seed begins to grow. A seed can't produce the harvest it's meant to yield unless it's connected to the source.

Source

So close to thee

From you I drink

Draw nigh to me

For he shall be like a tree planted by the waters, which spreads out its roots by the river, and will not fear when heat comes; But its leaf will be green and will not be anxious in the year of drought, nor will cease from yielding fruit. (Jeremiah 17:8 NKJV)

He shall be like a tree planted by the rivers of water, that brings forth its fruit in its season, whose leaf also shall not wither; and whatever he does shall prosper. (Psalms 1:3 NKJV)

Jeremiah compares us to "trees planted by the waters..." Every plant not only needs sunlight and pruning, they need water. What are you connected to? What is your source of life? The New Living Translation reads *"They are like trees planted along a riverbank, with roots that reach deep into the water. Such trees are not bothered by the heat or worried by long months of drought. Their leaves stay green, and they never stop producing fruit."(Jeremiah 17:8* NLT)

I want to make an emphasis on this part of the scripture, "with roots that reach deep into the water..." It bears witness with my spirit. What a great thing it is to be rooted and connected in Him. The Bible tells us in Ephesians 3:16-21 that we are to be rooted and grounded in love. We know that God is Love. He is the source of our strength and life. Everything we do is by the Holy Spirit. Jesus intentionally left us with a form of communication.

"If you love me, obey my commandments. And I will ask the Father, and he will give you another Advocate, who will never leave you. He is the Holy Spirit, who leads into all truth. The world cannot receive him, because it isn't looking for him and doesn't recognize him. But you know him, because he lives with you now and later will be in you. (John 14:15-17 NLT)

Allow a deepening to occur in Him. Be rooted and grounded in Him. He's your ultimate source: Root – Sheresh -- of people involving firmness or permanence. *In the same way you received Jesus our Lord and Messiah by faith, continue your journey of faith, progressing further into your union with him! Your spiritual roots go deeply into his life as you are continually infused with strength, encouraged in every way. For you are established in the faith you have absorbed and enriched by your devotion to him! (Colossians 2:6-7 TPT)*

Let me encourage you to chase after Jesus. Cling to Him and His word. Maybe there have been words spoken over you! Words spoken directly to your heart from Him that you need to remember and bring Him in remembrance of. Have you ever noticed when the Lord births revelation, a prophecy is released over your life? You might be like: "Lord, how is it that this person was all up in my prayer closet with me". How did they know? Haha. Well, we know it's the Holy Spirit. Here's where I'm going with this. Often times, moments like this happen and we get attacked with nonsense a week down the road. I'm convinced the Lord looks at us and thinks, "Did you already forget what I spoke?" We have to cling to the Word and the revelation that was released.

Timothy, my son, here are my instructions for you, based on the prophetic words spoken about you earlier. May they help you fight well in the Lord's battles. Cling to your faith in Christ and keep your conscience clear. For some people have deliberately violated their consciences; as a result, their faith has been shipwrecked. Hymenaeus and Alexander are two examples. I threw them out and handed them over to Satan so they might learn not to blaspheme God. (1 Timothy 1:18-20 NLT)

He is our source, He nurtures us. We stand upon Him; Jesus is our firm foundation.

Jesus replied, "If you only knew the gift God has for you and who you are speaking to, you would ask me, and I would give you living water." "But sir, you don't have a rope or a bucket," she said, "and this well is very deep. Where would you get this living water? And besides, do you think you're greater than our ancestor Jacob, who gave us this well? How can you offer better water than he and his sons and his animals enjoyed? Jesus replied, "Anyone who drinks this water will soon become thirsty again. But those who drink the water I give will never be thirsty again. It becomes a fresh, bubbling spring within them, giving them eternal life." (John 4:10-14 NLT)

Sometimes people question "Why do I have to go through this?" Why me, Lord? Resounding thoughts of most believers. We tend to think that we never have to go through stuff. We think life should just be peachy. Have y'all read the Bible that I read? Luke 2:1-16 portrays the birth of Jesus. When you read it, you will see that Jesus humbly came into this world, born of a virgin. His purpose was to restore us back to our original state, to bring restoration, reconcile us back to our Father (2 Corinthians 5:17-21). By doing that, Jesus Himself had to submit to the will of God and be crucified. He said to His Father,

If you are willing, please take this cup of suffering away from me. Yet I want your will to be done, not mine." Then an angel from heaven appeared and strengthened him. (Luke 22:42-43 NLT)

Reading that brings me great joy, as it should for you too, *"...Then an angel from heaven appeared and strengthened him."* The challenges we face always bring forth fruit, it's up to us as believers to yield to the process and understand that Jesus Himself hasn't neglected us and He never will with any process. He's not just the God of the beginning and end but the God of the process. He's intentional!

"So be strong and courageous! Do not be afraid and do not panic before them. For the Lord your God will personally go ahead of you. He will neither fail you nor abandon you." (Deuteronomy 31:6 NLT)

In January of 2020, I began twenty-one days of prayer and fasting. I started in the book of John. When I got to chapter 4, I was glued to this particular verse that said: He had to go through Samaria on the way. I asked the Lord, "Why did you have to go through there?" Jesus walked through Samaria, which means Guardianship. Guardianship means position of protecting or defending something. I've been on this journey with Jesus learning what He was up against, and what He had to walk through. Through it all His response was: I only do what the Father tells me, what I hear Him saying, what I see Him doing. The Humanity of Jesus, our perfect example of submission, He was fully God, and fully man. He knows you, He's walking with you, He's there for you.

And so, my journey began. I started to dwell on the word process. The Holy Spirit told me to open the notes app in my phone and search the word process. As it filtered through, I scrolled down to find a note labeled "Leadership" which held the notes to a class with Pastor Allen Hawes that I had taken while in Bible College. I had taken notes about the process that a seed goes through – birth, death, growth. The Lord cracked open a different realm in the Spirit for me. I started to see with different eyes. I had a revelation about how we have to walk through areas in our lives. We have to go through processes, but within any process He is very present and intentional. Weeks later I found myself sitting in a youth service. It was March 2020, and I was fresh out of revival meetings. The Lord told me to look up *John 12:24-26 TPT.*

"Let me make this clear: A single grain of wheat will never be more than a single grain of wheat unless it drops into the ground and dies. Because then it sprouts and

produces a great harvest of wheat—all because one grain died. "The person who loves his life and pampers himself will miss true life! But the one who detaches his life from this world and abandons himself to me, will find true life and enjoy it forever! If you want to be my disciple, follow me and you will go where I am going. And if you truly follow me as my disciple, the Father will shower his favor upon your life.

Birth

Born of a Virgin

By the very Ruach of God

Inhale His Spirit.

Exhale His Spirit.

Ruach flowing in my lungs.

I in Him, He in me – abide in me.

I started to see a picture of Jesus. Born of a virgin, coming into the world planted as a seed to die and bring forth fruit. His purpose on this earth was being born to die. Jesus is continually bearing fruit. Even though He is not walking the earth, His fruit still is.

Hebrews 12:2 reads "We do this by keeping our eyes on Jesus, the champion who initiates and perfects our faith. Because of the joy awaiting him, he endured the cross, disregarding its shame. Now he is seated in the place of honor beside God's throne."

Well people that joy was you and I. Thank God He sent His son Jesus giving us access to live a sin free life and tell others how to do so. He's the perfect picture of the process of a seed: Birth, Death, Growth.

This means that anyone who belongs to Christ has become a new person. The old life is gone; a new life has begun! (2 Corinthians 5:17 NLT)

God's created you with great purpose. I remember sitting in my old church's fellowship hall on a Wednesday night during youth service. Pastor Jackie was teaching. I felt impressed in my spirit to become a youth pastor. I told the Lord right then that I wanted to do what she was doing when I grow up. Little did I know that the Lord was calling me into the ministry. Having a new life in Christ birthed in me the desire to see a generation awakened. To see a life outside of myself. I wanted to be a part of something that was bigger than myself, something I couldn't do in my own strength. What does that look like for you?

And we know that God causes everything to work together for the good of those who love God and are called according to his purpose for them. (Romans 8:28 NLT)

It's according to His purpose for your life, throughout this process the Lord revealed to me my mandate for this generation. I always knew I was called to this generation but wasn't quite sure what that looked like. You see great men and women of God say my generation shall be shaken, which yes that's their mandate but I knew it was more than that for myself. The Lord birthed in me a mandate to see not only this generation encounter Jesus but generations to come.

"Let this be recorded for future generations, so that a people not yet born will praise the Lord." (Psalm 102:18 NLT)

As I read through the old testament, I noticed the message of Jesus being passed from one generation to the next, a goal to restore His people back to their original state. For instance,

After the death of Moses, the Lord's servant, the Lord spoke to Joshua son of Nun, Moses' assistant. He said, "Moses my servant is dead. Therefore, the time has come for you to lead these people, the Israelites, across the Jordan River into the land I am giving them. (Joshua 1:1-2 NLT)

Joshua learned from Moses, allowing Him to fully step into His call to lead the people.

Where does your journey begin? The moment you were physically born, or the moment you breathed in His spirit and accepted Him as Lord over your life, your savior? My friend, we call that salvation. Take time to stop and remember the time you asked the Lord to come into your heart. Internally, in the spirit that beautiful exchange happened. His death for your life. Did you actually stop and remember? If you haven't received that opportunity, I'd like to invite you to do so now. Repeat this prayer with your heart and lips out loud: Father, come and make my heart your home. Abide in me. Forgive me of my sin, wash me and cleanse me, set me free. I repent, turn my back on the world, and I run to you Jesus. Thank you for dying for me, I believe you're risen from the dead and coming back for me. I'm forgiven, I'm free, I dedicate my life to you this very day. In Jesus name, Amen. If you prayed that prayer, it's my highest honor to welcome you into the family, today starts the greatest journey with Jesus.

Imagine doing something new. Imagine having to learn, adjust, and change your way of doing things. For example, if you're trying to lose weight, and NO, I'm not saying you're fat, ha-ha. Losing weight requires you to exercise, change your eating habits, and fully commit to a healthy lifestyle. You'll never get the results that are entitled to you by exercising and eating healthy, unless you submit to change. You can't carry old habits into a new lifestyle. Stop eating the cheeseburger from Burger

King and eat the goodness of this Fresh Kitchen. Stepping into newness of life, a life with Jesus means we can't carry on the way we used to. The way we talk changes. The way we address people changes. The way we look at people changes. Even, the way we see Jesus and ourselves changes. In Galatians 5:24-25 we learn that we should nail our sinful passions to the cross and walk by the Spirit in every area of our life.

As he was approaching Damascus on this mission, a light from heaven suddenly shone down around him. 4 He fell to the ground and heard a voice saying to him, "Saul! Saul! Why are you persecuting me?"(Acts 9:3-4 NLT)

Even Saul fell to the ground, He went from persecuting Christians to preaching and teaching the gospel of Jesus Christ. One radical encounter with someone he used to despise led him to write 13 books in the New Testament. The Lord used him mightily. Paul couldn't keep his old nature and preach the gospel of Jesus Christ, the two don't mix. We're always required to submit ourselves to what His word says. Speaking and doing what He tells us by the Spirit. I can't count how many times the Holy Spirit has spoken something to me concerning my best friend. We could be miles away and it'll be spot on. I submitted to His will, to what He was speaking and in return she reaps the Lord being intentional. She is seen by Him so much that He put her on my spirit and told me to speak truths to her. Our greatest example of obedience is Jesus himself.

"So Jesus explained, "I tell you the truth, the Son can do nothing by himself. He does only what he sees the Father

doing. Whatever the Father does, the Son also does." (John 5:19 NLT)

"For I have come down from heaven to do the will of God who sent me, not to do my own will." (John 6:38 NLT)

"I don't speak on my own authority. The Father who sent me has commanded me what to say and how to say it. And I know his commands lead to eternal life; so, I say whatever the Father tells me to say." (John 12:49-50 NLT)

"But I will do what the Father requires of me, so that the world will know that I love the Father. Come, let's be going." (John 14:31 NLT)

If it's in His nature, it's for us.

Taste and see that the Lord is good! There are many flavors and aspects of Jesus we haven't even tapped into as believers. I imagine with any new area in our walk with Jesus we have to die to our way of doing things. Our will. For example, the amount of faith that you need to believe the Lord for five dollars would be different from the amount of faith you need to believe for five thousand dollars. We grow our faith never staying at the same level. Pick up your cross daily. Work your salvation out with fear and trembling. These are continuous actions in our lives that can bring us closer to Jesus. I'm reminded of the story when the Lord told Moses to take off His shoes because He was standing on Holy ground. That's such a great thing to picture. Your shoes – your way of walking. Take those shoes off so you can step into my goodness, you can step into me, for this is Holy ground.

Fast-forward to May 2020. I was already dealing with this issue, but it got out of control. My health had taken a turn for the worst. My flesh was being starved. I couldn't keep any type of food down. I couldn't even keep liquids down. I even tried to eat those squeeze baby food pouches and they wouldn't stay down. I was at war with myself and it affected everyone around me. I fasted, prayed, and went to healing school. Nothing was working in my favor. I began to grow bitter towards the Lord and couldn't understand why all of this was happening to me. One thing healing school, at the River at Tampa Bay Church, taught me was compassion. Once during a break, I was at the coffee cart and Pastor Allen Hawes and I were talking about youth ministry. He told me, "Bree, you hear me preach Matthew 9:36 all the time. How you have to have compassion. There will always be young people to preach to, but if you lack compassion you won't be effective." That same day, I headed back to healing school. The Pastor started teaching about compassion from Mark 3. He talked about how Jesus had compassion even on the Sabbath day and prayed for the man with the withered hand. It really ministered to my heart. I realized it doesn't matter what I'm going through He has so much compassion for me. He loves me and wants me healed. In that moment, the love and compassion of Jesus swept over me like none other.

After I attended healing school my health got worse.

I lost 20 pounds on top of the weight I intentionally lost at the beginning of the year. Can you say hangry?!! You know how crazy you get when you are hungry? Well, I was that… times ten. It affected everything. Just like cancer spreads throughout a body, my health issues seemed to spread to everything and everyone I was around. My whole demeanor changed. I was miserable.

"While Jesus was here on earth, he offered prayers and pleadings, with a loud cry and tears, to the one who could rescue him from death. And God heard his prayers because of his deep reverence for God. Even though Jesus was God's Son, he learned obedience from the things he suffered. In this way, God qualified him as a perfect High Priest, and he became the source of eternal salvation for all those who obey him." (Hebrews 5:7-9 NLT)

In June I took a trip to PA to clear my head. I thought having a change of people and scenery would help. I was actually just left with my thoughts, so it did nothing. I was still stuck with all my questions. Why am I going through this? What is happening? One night I received a message about suffering. It's not a common topic to talk about and I honestly could care less what people think. There are lessons to learn in suffering, the scriptures I just wrote back that up.

Stronger Greek Dictionary 3958 Pascho: defines suffering: apparently a primary verb; to experience a sensation or impression (usually painful): -- feel, passion, suffer, vex.

"To experience," "to go through", "to endure": *I have suffered many things this day in a dream because of him" (Matthew 27:19). A woman "had suffered many things of many physicians" (Mark 5:26).* Other common phrases are *"to suffer affliction" (See:1 Thess 3:4, Hebrews 11:25)*

Jesus learned obedience; this scripture alone touched my heart. The one I look to for everything suffered and was taught through His suffering, and that qualified Him. Now that's a different perspective, I've been qualified by the Lord through my suffering because of the things I've learned. He doesn't call the qualified, He qualifies the called, you are the called. In your suffering, in your learning, He's preparing you for your purpose.

To suffer, has many different meanings. Some happen to you and some you choose. Jesus had an option but took on suffering for us. As we follow Jesus there will be times you suffer but know that our suffering will not last and we will grow and mature in Him. There's so much beauty to discover in the beautiful mess of suffering. Yeah, you might think I'm crazy for calling suffering beautiful. While you're in it it's messy, once you get through it you look back and carry foundational truths about Jesus that will carry you for the rest of your life. Hence the reason why I'm even writing this book. The Lord has intended great purpose for you. If you've ever been through a time of suffering, or you're going through this process, I want you to take a look and ask the Lord to open your eyes to the spirit. Ask Him to open your ears to hear what He's speaking, and what He's showing you.

Hebrew 5:7-9 changed me, it allowed me to see Jesus once again with different eyes. The eyes of my spirit were enlightened to this word. Jesus had authority on the cross. He could have called out to God to save him from the suffering, but He didn't. *"For the joy that was set before Him..."* *(Hebrews 12)*. It's from those dark valley's that strength begins to form, as we submit ourselves in obedience to His process. I guarantee you whether it's good, bad, or ugly, if you just stop and listen, He's speaking.

We are His sheep, and we hear His voice, we can't fall to the voice of the enemy. The voice of a stranger I will not follow. (John 10:27 NLT)

That's key in life. If it's not Him, don't follow it. Insecurity, fear, doubt, unbelief, and comparison are not the voice of God. Love, peace, boldness, courage, kindness, and faithfulness are His voice. We need to be familiar with the nature of our Father. Our identity and way of life is wrapped up in Him. Acts 17:28 tells us: *In Him we live, and move, and have our being.* How much more do we need to know the sound of the Father's voice and His nature? This word is timely, the media will spew garbage, friends and family will speak fear, but what is Papa saying? What are you feeding your spirit with? The word and faith or fear, doubt, and unbelief? It's time to be still, draw near and identify His voice above the stranger.

"But the true Shepherd walks right up to the gate, and because the gatekeeper knows who he is, he opens the gate and lets him in. And the sheep recognize the voice of

the true Shepherd, for he calls his own by name and leads them out for they belong to him. And when he has brought out all his sheep, he walks ahead of them and they follow him, for they are familiar with his voice. But they will run away from strangers and never follow them because they know it's the voice of a stranger." (John 10:2-5 TPT)

This process is one I'll remember for the rest of my life, it marked me in the natural, and in the Spirit. I've seen great men and women of God who serve the Lord, hear from Him, obedient, in full time ministry, people who legit walk with the Lord. They've laid hands on the sick and seen them recover yet they have sickness, pain, or disease in their body. They literally need a miracle in their body. So, in my mind it didn't make sense. In my mind, I questioned healing. God's not afraid of our questions, in fact those questions drew me closer to Him. I've heard many stories. I've personally prayed for people and seen them healed. I kept thinking to myself, and telling Hailée: "If He can't heal them why would He heal me? Because clearly, I'm not being healed right now." I want you to know that His hand is not too short to reach you. When you're weak, the Lord can show up strong on your behalf. He fights for us when we can't fight for ourselves. He is strong and makes us strong.

Each time he said, "My grace is all you need. My power works best in weakness." So now I am glad to boast about my weaknesses, so that the power of Christ can work through me. That's why I take pleasure in my weaknesses, and in the insults, hardships, persecutions, and troubles that I suffer for Christ. For when I am weak, then I am strong. (2 Corinthians 12:9-10 NLT)

I almost walked away from the Lord. It wasn't lack of faith, although the enemy led me to believe it was, I had faith then and I have faith now. I was being challenged to change my perspective. The Lord was pulling me in through this attack on my body. Imagine yourself planting a seed in the ground, in the soil, that's a picture of humility to me. May I go low so He can be exalted high.

"He must become greater and greater, and I must become less and less." (John 3:30 NLT)

"So it's necessary for him to increase and for me to be diminished."(John 3:30 TPT)

Due to hospital rules, I was only allowed one visitor the entire week. Because so many people work, it was just me and the Lord for a few days and He "snatched" me. No visitors, no family, no friends. I died to my thoughts, doubts, and unbelief. I fully submitted myself to the Lord, opened His word to Psalm 27 and read it every day. I had worship music playing daily and when it was time to sleep, I played Kenneth Hagin healing scriptures. A transformation began. His word was penetrating my heart, going where a knife of a man couldn't go.

"For the word of God is alive and powerful. It is sharper than the sharpest two-edged sword, cutting between soul and spirit, between joint and marrow. It exposes our innermost thoughts and desires."(Hebrews 4:12 NLT)

I was then a seed fallen to the ground, in that rich soil of His presence, learning of Him, His goodness, dying to myself and what I thought I knew. God never put that sickness on me. His word never changed. I was the one who had to SUBMIT, and change. I find it funny that people blame God and put Him in a box. This is why, in the introduction, I encouraged you to open up your spirit. Our natural carnal mind will always shut God out. I've done it and now I find myself telling the Lord, "May I never put you in a box. May I experience you in your fullness." Stop comparing your situation to someone else's. Yes, it's the same word but the Lord is so aware of you. He knows how you respond. The way He speaks to you is different. The relationship you have with Jesus is unique. Be okay with that. I've found within this process my faith has grown. Just because I can't see it and my carnal mind doesn't understand it, that leaves room for me to lean in on Jesus more. I trust in Him. I trust who He says He is, not what my mind says He's supposed to be and do and how He should do it. Ultimately it isn't up to me. I need to trust the process and the one who walks me through it. Guys, I encourage you to read the story of Lazarus. Jesus went to his tomb after he died and called him out. My dude got up and walked out of the tomb. Let God do what He does best in your life too. The more time you spend with someone, the more you learn their character. You learn how they act, respond, and what they like and don't like. When I know someone and have a relationship with them, I CAN TRUST THEM. Jesus walked with me, and I trusted Him the moment I submitted to His will for my life. But only because I'd spent time with Him. Outside of my relationship with Jesus, my relationship with my best friend is prime example. We've spent so much time together that I trust her with my whole life. I know if something goes down, if something exciting happens, I'm calling or texting her. Think of those people in your life that you know no matter what, I can trust this person. That's who Jesus is to us, unwavering, consistent, faithful. Moments like these are very teachable times if you allow them to be. They're actually pretty beautiful. My friend once said, "What's beautiful about a man like you is that you raise the dead and had to suffer too, Jesus."

The Lily of the Valley, the one who came and dwelled with me in my mess, the one who's waiting to enter into yours. I researched the Lily of the Valley. It's an actual flower that is sustained in cool temperatures. It grows in the cool of the day. There's beauty in the valley, so much is cultivated there, from the Father's heart. Above all else, can I tell you that you don't have to stay in your valley. He's very present and wants to teach you and lift you out of it. What Harvest is awaiting you on the other side of your process? Don't wait! Stop going through the motions. Be still and know He's God and let Him be God.

Pray this prayer modeled after Proverbs 4:20-23 TPT: Father, help me pay attention to your sayings. Let my thoughts be filled with your words. Let them penetrate deep into my spirit. Imparting true life and radiant health into the very core of my being. Above all else, I'll guard the affections of my heart for they affect all that I am. I'll pay attention to the welfare of my innermost being, for out of it flows the issues of life. I thank you now more than ever I can hear your voice clearly concerning myself and others. Thank you for always leading and guiding me into all truth and raising me up to be a voice within this generation. In Jesus name, Amen.

The only thing stopping me from fully entering into what the Lord was trying to teach me about Himself was me. Pride was rooted in me at a very young age, I always closed myself off from help whether that was from the Lord or people. I never wanted anyone to know what I was going through, I always had to be tough and make it seem like everything was okay when actually it wasn't.

And he gives grace generously. As the Scriptures say, "God opposes the proud but gives grace to the humble." (James 4:6 NLT)

There's a key in this verse, "gives grace to the humble". The moment we humble ourselves before the Lord and stop putting on this front that says: "I can do bad all by myself" or "I can carry this weight alone" His grace comes right on in. I remember lying in the hospital bed telling the Lord I was fully present and ready to work with Him. That's when everything started to change. Grace is His ability, His strength to prevail. John writes in *Chapter 15: Apart from Jesus, he can do nothing.* This is how we ought to live our lives. What area in your life haven't you fully submitted to the Lord that could possibly be blocking your process? Don't allow pride to steal your gift, rather allow the Lord to give you grace to walk through by submitting yourself to His process.

After surgery I recovered at my best friends for a week. Soon after, I was feeling defeated and miserable and felt led to read from one of my Cultivate Books titled "The Clarity Winter Brings". I had a few pages left but I flipped to the back and read "The winter is your deepening; the winter is your gift." I began weeping in an instant. I said to the Lord, "You know what, you're right". He reminded me of John 4 and how He had been trying to tell me all along I was about to walk through this, I was numb. I shut Him out but He was right there with me on the other side of the door. So that was the answer to my question of why. The Lord spoke to my heart "Bree, I had to go through Samaria just like you had to go through your process. I needed to teach you I'm here in the process so don't shut me out. My intentions for you are always good. I needed you to experience my love and compassion for you, because you can't give out what you don't have. The very nature of Jesus was so present, I received a great gift to experience Him at a greater level, as my friend, as a father, as the lily of the valley, the one who never leaves nor forsakes me. Man, I'm crying now as I write these words just thinking of His goodness. Thinking of His hand that kept me and strengthened me. I couldn't do it alone; my best friend, Hailée was by my side through it all, along with many others. She came home this same night, knocked on my door, and visited with me. I told her the Lord gave me my why. Why I had to go through this process. Why I had to learn some things that I wouldn't have learned, and how the Lord completely unraveled the process of a seed with all of it. She began to cry with me.

When he saw the crowds, he had compassion on them because they were confused and helpless, like sheep without a shepherd. (Matthew 9:36 NLT)

Now listen, I'm no farmer. I'm no pro at this. In the natural it may not always make sense. With the birth of a seed, I always think about Jesus, especially in the book of John. Our life is to reflect Jesus.

Death

Fallen seed — crucified hung on a tree.
Ascending and descending.
Restoration began

Filling the entire universe with Himself.

Let this be known
We'll never be more
unless we fall to the ground and die.

Planted as Seed
Buried beneath
Raised to new life, we were found.

Submerged in Him.
Breaking through the light.
Cultivating in me the need to be nurtured
by the one true King.

Hebrews 12:2 "...for the joy that was set before Him He endured the cross."
Philippians 2:12 NKJV Therefore, my beloved, as you have always obeyed, not as in my presence only, but now much more in my absence, work out your own salvation with fear and trembling.

Let's break this down. *Jesus is the Word. John 1:1, the Word is a seed John 8:11* Therefore, when Jesus (word-seed) died, He was buried in the ground, and rose to life. God so loved the world that He gave His only begotten son. Generations are attached to this beautiful exchange. He was the seed that was buried and raised to bring forth fruit. That fruit is you and me from generation to generation. You've heard it said, you can count the seed in an apple, but you can't count the apples in a seed. I was listening to Rick Pino and he said something that caught my attention. "One generation was faithful with a seed so the next generation could eat of its fruit." Jesus was faithful with His process. His call. He knew His purpose on this earth and He was willing to die so we could have the fruit of freedom, a sin free life. Are you willing to be faithful with yourself? We are the seed that has to die to self, to bear fruit. Are you willing to be faithful with your walk with Jesus, and walk through some stuff? There are people attached to your walk that only you can reach. I can't reach them for you. I may never meet the people you'll meet. Your willingness to die to self, your willingness to learn of the nature of Jesus and be like Him is important. Paul tells us to imitate me as I imitate Christ. *Genesis 1:27 tells us: He made man in His image, man and women alike.* We must be a seed that's willing to die to self so we can produce fruit, so generations to come can eat of it.

During a service when someone taught on the goodness of God. Laying there with my face on the floor allowing the Lord to minister to me. I proceeded to get up and sit in my seat, tears streaming down my face. Pastor Jeff Hughes asked, "Where's Bree? I know she was laid out." He found me and prayed over me. He said, "The Lord knows you're a seed willing to die." These words hit my spirit like a ton of bricks. The Lord was confirming everything He had spoken to me. It's an honor to die to my flesh daily. His purpose and plan has been placed in me for such a time as this, it is the same for you too. I'll preach the gospel to my generation for generations to come. I've now found my purpose here on earth. I can't do that with my flesh in the way. I can only do it by His Spirit, by His nature. We all know 1 Corinthians 13 talks about the Love of God. I'm afraid we have forgotten that without that love (His character) we can do nothing. We're just a loud noise of religion, not being effective for the Kingdom. I want to be known for pouring out His love. Not just some noise that didn't even touch the heart of a young person. So yes, I'll choose death to my ways, my flesh, and cling to Jesus. Will you?

Hailée Perspective

"I knew Bree was going through some tough things for a few months. Very intense health things. To see it from an outside perspective really impacted me and affected me. It was a lot to go through, and I know Bree doesn't really like talking about it. I know it's hard for her to tell you all of this because it was a difficult time. She lost around 18 pounds because she was unable to eat. I would talk to her and I knew this wasn't the happy, funny, Bree. I had picked her up from the hospital one Saturday for her to come recover at my house. She and I were reading the Cultivate Books at the same time although not on purpose. I had already read the part in the book talking about the winter is your deepening, the winter is your gift. When I picked her up that day, that sentence kept replaying in my heart. I kept hearing the Lord say the winter is your deepening, the winter is your gift. He impressed upon me, "I didn't rob her of anything. This was a gift for her that I was about to use to teach her about myself and my nature."

He was showing me a lot of things that were blooming in her heart in a season that could seem so barren. In a season that could seem so full of death.

There was so much life that the Lord was creating inside of her. He had repeated the sentence to me while we were riding but I didn't feel the need to particularly tell her at that time. Wednesday night she told me the Lord had showed her this. I said, "Bree, this is exactly what the Lord had showed me on Saturday while riding in the car. The sentence kept repeating in my head. Telling you wouldn't have had the same effect as the Lord telling you because it comes directly from His heart." I began to cry because it was such a confirmation how present the Lord is. He's so present. He was there the entire time through every conversation we had and every question she had. He was so present in that. I remember telling her that I knew she was going to be okay physically. I knew she was going to be fine. I knew she was going to be taken care of. I knew she was going to be able to eat again. My loudest prayer in her season wasn't that she was going to be healed physically, that was a given, my loudest prayer was that her heart wouldn't miss what the Lord was doing. It's just beautiful to see the fruit of it.

I remember if I had questions about something as a child, my Dad would take me out, he would talk to me, he would talk to me until I understood until I got what would answer them and if I didn't get it, he would keep talking until I understood the answers to my questions. I felt like she was telling me all this and it was like the Father was saying, "You're good, you got it, you got what I was trying to tell you. Not to say the Lord put these things on her. I believe it was just an attack on her body. It was beautiful to see the scripture work in her life. Especially the scripture that tells us He turns all things for the good of those that love Him. Even in the midst of this deep darkness: emotionally, spiritually, and physically. Even in the midst of every-thing coming against her. The Lord did something so good. It was so fruitful. When I saw her on Wednesday, I saw the real Bree. Full of compassion. She received a larger capacity to have and show compassion. God was faithful to Bree. When I wasn't in the hospital with her, He was. When I didn't know the pain that she was feeling in her heart, He did. When I wasn't close, He was. He was a faithful friend." In the end, I would see the Lord's goodness, faithfulness, kindness, and His friendship. He would tell me Bree was going to be okay. I saw the goodness of God through something that seemed so horrible, something that seemed so full of death. He brought so much life and fruit to her. I saw Bree coming alive in ways I hadn't before. I saw so many of the things she had spoken and talked about the Lord become so real to her.

I had Hailée share her perspective one night during church because it's one thing for me to tell you, but it's another when someone on the outside looking in tells you. Through the attack on my health, as you've read, Jesus didn't rob me of anything. He gave me Himself; He gave me His nature. He gave me His compassion. He gave me His eyes and made me His mouthpiece. In that beautifully messy process came fruit. I grew and saw sides of Him I never would have if I didn't finally submit my life to Him. I could have easily shut Him out and grown cold towards Him. Blamed Him for my issues even. But I welcomed Him in, took His invitation, and walked through it with Him. What process are you avoiding today? What do you feel like you're being robbed of? Jesus is calling you out and pulling you in. He's asking you to come away with Him and learn of Him. He wants you to know that He's not only God when you are on the mountain top but He's also the Lily of the Valley.

Your purpose is hidden, *"And he said unto them, is a candle brought to be put under a bushel, or under a bed? and not to be set on a candlestick? For there is nothing hid, which shall not be manifested; neither was anything kept secret, but that it should come abroad. If any man has ears to hear, let him hear. (Mark 4:21-23 KJV)*

And he said unto them, take heed what ye hear: with what measure ye mete, it shall be measured to you: and unto you that hear shall more be given." (Mark 4:24 KJV)

Here Christ makes clear that previously unrevealed truth will be completely revealed so that all can see it alike. Here we have a warning as to what we hear and a promise that if we hear aright more will be given. If we reject truth what we have will be taken away. Be willing to submit to the process and allow the Lord to show you hidden truths not only about Him, but about Him according to your plans and purpose. There's so much potential within you Jesus is ready to work with. Remember, you are not alone. The Lord is present and willing to walk with you. I recently wrote a message about the Father being aware of you.

"You are so intimately aware of me, Lord. You read my heart like an open book and you know all the words I'm about to speak before I even start a sentence! You know every step I will take before my journey even begins." (Psalm 139:3-4 TPT)

To even know that He's aware of us we have to stop and become aware of Him and His presence, allowing Him to speak to our hearts. *Come seek ye my face, my heart said to thee, Lord thy face I'll seek (Psalm 27).* In His inviting we open up our hearts to Him, allowing Him to come and cultivate something beautiful in our death. I just love to be saturated in Him. *It's because of Him I live and move and have my being Acts 17:28.* In

His presence I am restored back to my original state, knowing my God given purpose so I can be effective and impact a life for Jesus. That's what this is really about. To be so much like Him, calling forth the seed in others to come alive.

Let me make this clear: A single grain of wheat will never be more than a single grain of wheat unless it drops into the ground and dies. Because then it sprouts and produces a great harvest of wheat—all because one grain died. The person who loves his life and pampers himself will miss true life! But the one who detaches his life from this world and abandons himself to me, will find true life and enjoy it forever! If you want to be my disciple, follow me and you will go where I am going. And if you truly follow me as my disciple, the Father will shower his favor upon your life. (John 12:24-26 TPT)

In October 2020, I had the opportunity to attend Light A Candle Trip to Washington, DC for Let Us Worship with Sean Feucht. One afternoon we stopped in Georgetown to grab a late lunch before our next outreach. As soon as we got inside the restaurant a lady tells us we need to stand 6 feet apart. I looked around and said, "Is she talking to us?" It made no sense in my mind because we came in as a group and had been doing life together all week. I got a little annoyed, but we spread apart anyway. After we ordered our food, we went outside to eat. We sat on top of the tables because there were no chairs. The lady also came outside, and I thought she was going to say something about us sitting outside so close to each other. Instead, she asked if we would take a photo of us eating together and tag them on social media. "It's so nice to see you outside with no chairs during this time." We were running behind schedule, so we quickly finished up our lunch and headed out. As we were walking away, I felt in my spirit to pray for her. I told the Lord I can't go back and pray for her because we are late already, and we have to go. It was at the moment that my friend Ivan spoke up. He said, "We need to go pray for her". Wow! So, Ivan and I went back. We went in and asked her if we could pray for her. She said of course, I would love for you to pray for me. My Mom and I used to pray before every meal, so I'll take prayer anytime someone offers it to me. I asked her if there was anything specific she needed prayer for because the hand of God was on her. Her face was radiating.

She responded by telling us that a year ago today I should have been dead. She was hit by a drunk driver. She had a concussion. It was literally a life and death situation. With tears streaming down her face, I told her the Lord sent me here to DC just for her. It's not a coincidence nor a happenstance that I met you and the Lord told me to come pray for you. The Lord chose to send someone to pray for you on your one-year anniversary of that horrible accident. I prayed a prayer of blessing and protection over her. I told her the hand of God was on her life. I told her that she had pulled away from Him in the past but today was her day to fix that. She repeated this prayer with me. Dear Lord

Jesus, come into my heart. Forgive me of my sins. Wash me and cleanse me.

Just like that, I crucified my flesh, pushed aside MY agenda for God's agenda. Jesus had purpose that day. If I didn't yield to His purpose, that lady wouldn't have that gift on the anniversary of her near-death experience. She had an experience with God, all because a seed was willing to fall to the ground and die. In that moment I realized you have to die daily to your plans, your flesh's desire, and be led by the Spirit instead.

Those who belong to Christ Jesus have nailed the passions and desires of their sinful nature to his cross and crucified them there. Since we are living by the Spirit, let us follow the Spirit's leading in every part of our lives. (Galatians 5:24-25 NLT)

Now let's get a little nerdy here to give you a natural view. I began studying seed germination: Environmental conditions have to be favorable for germination to occur. The environmental conditions must be favorable in order to support the growing plant. The soil depth, amount of water, and temperature are all critical conditions that must be met in order for the process of germination to be initiated. Typically, the soil conditions must be moist and warm.

Water imbibition: When environmental conditions are optimal, germination is initiated by a process termed water imbibition. The seed absorbs water through a structure called a micropyle, which induces swelling of the seed until it splits open.

Root and Shoot formation: Once the seed has

ruptured, the radicle (primary root) and plumule (shoot) can emerge from the seed. This process is initiated by specific enzymes that become activated when the seed is exposed to water. The roots grow downwards, and the shoot grows upwards towards the soil surface.

A seedling is formed: Once the shoot emerges from the soil surface, the cotyledons become fully unfolded and expand, eventually forming the first leaves. Once this occurs, the plant is ready to initiate photosynthesis and is considered a seedling.

You might read that and wonder what it this even talking about. I'll break it down. You have to posture yourself to be in the presence of God (environment) You have to surround yourself with people who have the same goal as you which is to serve Jesus. You become like the people you hang around. Spend time in the secret place. Put yourself around people who are going to encourage you and always point you to Jesus. This is where the old man dies off. As you cultivate your time with Jesus you start to go through a cleansing process. He washes you of your old nature and you start to reflect Him. As the seed ruptures, you're able to grow roots down deep into the soil, staying connected to the source. Within this "death experience" you spring forth life and bear fruit. Not just within yourself but in the kingdom also. Producing Kingdom fruit. He's the perfect gardener. Tending to our hearts and cutting off what doesn't belong. He wants to make us like Him.

Growth

I'm a tree planted by the water

Producing fruit in every season

Never wavering

Connected to the source.

I am the grapevine

My Father is the gardener

Bringing forth multitudes, you and me alike.

What causes' growth is your willingness to allow the Lord to prune you. The Holy Spirit reminded me of another Cultivate Book series titled "The Head to The Heart Journey". There's a passage in there called "Discovering God's Goodness". It speaks of the orange groves they visited in Florida. "As we stumbled over ant hills with juice-stained faces and sticky hands, our new friend explained that many young orange trees must be exhaustively pruned for the first few years of their lives to ensure maturity and to sustain long-term growth. Often times, an orange tree sapling will focus all of its energy and nutrients on bearing fruit in a young state, before it has reached full maturity. In striving to produce fruit, the immature tree will starve itself of the nutrients it so desperately needs to develop. It will die long before it's time. Lee, a wise farmer, knows that the anxious young tree must be pruned back until it has learned the way to yield. In love, he teaches the tree what it cannot teach itself. I propose that if we are too known and recognized by our fruit, then just like the orange tree, we must yield ourselves to our heavenly Father, to be pruned so that we may mature, sustain long-term growth and produce fruit. This is an invitation to growth unlike anything we have ever known." I want to invite you into growth. Ask Him what area's in my life need pruning? Jesus calls us to cultivate a fruitful life.

"I am the true grapevine, and my Father is the gardener. He cuts off every branch of mine that doesn't produce fruit, and he prunes the branches that do bear fruit so they will produce even more. You have already been pruned and purified by the message I have given you. Remain in me, and I will remain in you. For a branch cannot produce fruit if it is severed from the vine, and you cannot be fruitful unless you remain in me. "Yes, I am the vine; you are the branches. Those who remain in me, and I in them, will produce much fruit. For apart from me you can do nothing. Anyone who does not remain in me is thrown away like a useless branch and withers. Such branches are gathered into a pile to be burned. But if you remain in me and my words remain in you, you may ask for anything you want, and it will be granted! When you produce much fruit, you are my true disciples. This brings great glory to my Father. "I have loved you even as the Father has loved me. Remain in my love. When you obey my commandments, you remain in my love, just as I obey my Father's commandments and remain in his love. I have told you these things so that you will be filled with my joy. Yes, your joy will overflow! This is my commandment: Love each other in the same way I have loved you. There is no greater love than to lay down one's life for one's friends. You are my friends if you do what I command. I no longer call you slaves, because a master doesn't confide in his slaves. Now you are my friends, since

I have told you everything the Father told me. You didn't choose me. I chose you. I appointed you to go and produce lasting fruit, so that the Father will give you whatever you ask for, using my name. This is my command: Love each other. (John 15:1-17 NLT)

The Greek word for abide is meno. It conveys a place of profound connectedness to Jesus. We need to stay in Him, dwell in Him, remain steadfast in Him. Faithfully continue in Him. The Father prunes, shapes, and tends to every branch. He nurtures each one to be healthy and produce fruit. This causes us to experience intimacy and enduring fruitfulness. Many people are living with unsettled souls in this restless world. I was one of them. Jesus invites us to unpack our bags and settle our souls. Jesus is the only way to experience a life that's truly fruitful and joyful. I benefit from knowing who God is and I want that for you too.

A call to examine your heart as the Psalmist David wrote *"Search me, O God, and know my heart; test me and know my anxious thoughts. Point out anything in me that offends you and lead me along the path of everlasting life"* (Psalm 139:23-24 NLT)

To keep anything alive you always need a good environment to cultivate in. What are you feeding yourself spiritually? Who are you hanging around? Check your surroundings my friend. As I went through the pruning process in that hospital, the Lord showed me His nature, I would read through and through the book of John and cultivate a beautiful connection with Him. Never neglect the secret place, your time with

Him is far more important than some birthday party or having to please others by showing your face. He will give you the grace to say no when you need to say no. When the Lord calls you away to be with Him, take my advice and GO! The very thing your spirit needs to sustain you is found in His presence. There's been times in my life I've neglected the secret place and the fruit of my life spoke of it. Everything seemed to fall apart. Another thing I would caution you about is to be careful what you watch, entertain, and the words of your mouth. Staying mindful of who you spend time with.

"Bad company corrupts good character." (1 Corinthians 15:33 NLT)

"Your eye is like a lamp that provides light for your body. When your eye is healthy, your whole body is filled with light. But when your eye is unhealthy, your whole body is filled with darkness. And if the light you think you have is actually darkness, how deep that darkness is! "No one can serve two masters. For you will hate one and love the other; you will be devoted to one and despise the other. You cannot serve God and be enslaved to money. (Matthew 6:22-24 NLT)

The tongue can bring death or life; those who love to talk will reap the consequences. (Proverbs 18:21 NLT)

There were actions I needed to do to sustain this growth, such as daily devotion, prayer, setting aside intentional time with the Lord. I started to notice as I connected with Jesus and took on His nature, certain people began to disappear from my life. The Bible says:

"Be ye Holy as I am Holy." We are to pursue holiness in our lives. Holy means to be set apart. If you're ever going to produce fruit for Jesus, you have to be set apart with Him. We need to dwell in the house of the Lord all the days of our life. This is the kind of environment we're called to.

If you try to hang on to your life, you will lose it. But if you give up your life for my sake, you will save it. (Matthew 16:25 NLT)

One Sunday morning during service, Pastor Caleb Ring was going throughout the congregation praying for people and came to me. He said, "You haven't seen anything yet Bree, you haven't felt anything yet, eye has not seen, ear has not heard, what the Lord God has instore for you." That was May 31st, 2020, and friends that prayer was spot on. But I'll tell you this, nothing in the Kingdom of God is ever handed to you. You always have to be willing to do your part. I still haven't seen or experienced everything the Lord has instore for me, but the greatest thing about that is the processes I'll continue to go through to learn and experience more. Knowing it's not in my strength, my power, nor my wisdom. Everything I've obtained or will obtain will come from the Father. Through my submitting and trusting of His way. Taking up my cross daily. Webster's defines the word process as: a series of actions or steps taken to achieve a particular end. There's no greater process then this: Birth, Death, and Growth. That's the seed within every believer that has the potential to produce fruit. You are that seed, and that seed is within you. As believers, the process we go through is continual. The Bible instructs us to die to ourselves and our natural way of thinking in order to grow and bear fruit. Every believer has the potential to grow. It's what you do with your potential that counts. I charge you today to submit to the process. Die to yourself, and be about your Father's business, It's the message of Jesus throughout every generation that reached you. You have the opportunity to walk with Jesus in your process and discover who He is and your hidden purpose within His nature. As I've reflected many times upon this journey, I realized in order for things to live they must die first. He's calling you to go a little deeper with Him. Initially this life we live isn't about us, it's about our willingness to submit to His will and bring others the same opportunity. Let's return the favor. "May the Lamb that was slain receive the reward of His suffering." - The Moravians